TEACHER TIME-SAVERS

70+ REPRODUCIBLES FOR ALL OCCASIONS

By
Stevan Krajnjan

Good Apple

Editor: Jeri Cipriano

Good Apple, Inc.
A Division of Frank Schaffer Publications
23740 Hawthorne Blvd.
Torrance, CA 90505-5927

7 8 9 MAL 01 00 99 98

CONTENTS

INTRODUCTION

Teaching is a rewarding, challenging, and sometimes stressful profession. Because teachers work in demanding environments and must perform numerous tasks, often simultaneously, organizational tools are helpful. We all know that time is one of the teacher's most precious commodities—every minute saved translates directly into more time available for planning or interacting with students.

The reproducibles in *Teacher Time-Savers* have been designed specifically to help teachers save time and reduce their daily work loads. Included are many practical and attractive charts, forms, checklists, tables, calendars, lesson plan guides, and reference pages. You may wish to make copies of selected pages to keep in file folders. Or you may prefer to make your own customized resource in a three-ring binder. Duplicate as many pages of each format as you need to accommodate your schedule, class size, or other needs.

No matter what your teaching assignment, you are sure to find plenty of useful ideas and reproducibles in *Teacher Time-Savers.*

CLASS LIST

TEACHER .... CLASS .... ROOM ....

Name	Phone No.	Date of Birth	Age	Locker Number/Combination

DIAGNOSTIC TESTING

SUBJECT OF TESTING						
TYPE OF TEST GIVEN						
DATE OF TEST						
NAME						

TEACHER TIMETABLE

TEACHER .... CLASS .... ROOM ....

Period	Day 1	Day 2	Day 3	Day 4	Day 5	Day 6

TODAY'S LESSON PLAN

DAY .... DATE ....

PERIOD .... CLASS .... ROOM	SUPPLIES NEEDED

ASSIGNED HOMEWORK :

PHOTOCOPY:

PERIOD .... CLASS .... ROOM	SUPPLIES NEEDED

ASSIGNED HOMEWORK :

PHOTOCOPY:

SUPERVISION DUTIES:

STAFF MEETINGS

DATE	NOTES

REMINDER:

DATE	NOTES

REMINDER:

DATE	NOTES

REMINDER:

NOTES:

PARENT COMMUNICATIONS

Name of Parent	Date	Discussion	Outcome

© 1996 Good Apple

PARENT INTERVIEWS

Student:

Parent Interviewed: Date:

Comments:

Follow-up:

Student:

Parent Interviewed: Date:

Comments:

Follow-up:

Student:

Parent Interviewed: Date:

Comments:

Follow-up:

A NOTE TO:

FROM:

DATE:

A NOTE TO:

FROM:

DATE:

A NOTE TO:

FROM:

DATE:

A NOTE TO:

FROM:

DATE:

Thank You

Thank You

Thank You

Thank You

THINGS TO DO ✔

1.
2.
3.
4.
5.
6.
7.
8.
9.
10.
11.
12.
13.
14.
15.
16.
17.
18.
19.
20.

THINGS TO DO ✔

THINGS TO DO ✔

1.	
2.	
3.	
4.	
5.	
6.	
7.	
8.	
9.	
10.	
11.	
12.	
13.	
14.	
15.	
16.	
17.	
18.	
19.	
20.	

1.	
2.	
3.	
4.	
5.	
6.	
7.	
8.	
9.	
10.	
11.	
12.	
13.	
14.	
15.	
16.	
17.	
18.	
19.	
20.	

FROM THE DESK OF

_____

ASSIGNMENT RECORD

CLASS: _____

PERIOD: _____

STUDENT NAME

ASSIGNMENT

HOMEWORK COMPLETION RECORD

TEACHER .... CLASS ....

NAME	TYPE OF HOMEWORK / DUE DATE					

MONTH .... YEAR ....

SUNDAY	MONDAY	TUESDAY	WEDNESDAY	THURSDAY	FRIDAY	SATURDAY

OUR BIRTHDAYS

NAME	DATE OF BIRTH	NAME	DATE OF BIRTH

LEAVING THE ROOM

CLASS ....

Date	Student Name	Time (Out)	Time (In)

EQUIPMENT CHECKLIST

BECOME WELL ORGANIZED BY BRINGING THE FOLLOWING TO CLASS.

✔

1.
2.
3.
4.
5.
6.
7.
8.

✔

9.
10.
11.
12.
13.
14.
15.
16.

17. POSITIVE ATTITUDE ✔

OUR GOALS

1. Be well organized.

2. Always work hard.

3. Use our time efficiently.

4. Be on time.

5. Be kind and polite.

6. Finish all work on time.

7. Be helpful to those who need help.

8. Be patient.

9. Be forgiving.

10. Avoid senseless arguments.

11. Wait our turn to speak.

12. Raise our hands before asking questions.

13. Treat others the way we would like

 to be treated.

Improve students' organizational skills by helping them keep track of assignments. Cut along dotted line and invite students to glue the homework strip on the insides of their binders.

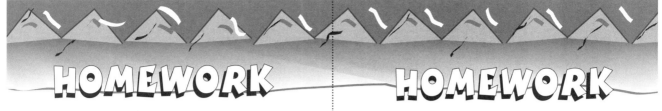

HOMEWORK

Date	Subject & Homework	Due Date	✔

HOMEWORK

Date	Subject & Homework	Due Date	✔

About Me!

My name is _____

Some people also call me _____

My present address is _____

_____

These are my family members _____

_____

My present telephone number is _____

I was born on _____

I like _____

_____

I dislike _____

I have a special friend whose name is _____

Things that I do well are _____

I spend a lot of time _____

This year I would like to learn about _____

I would be better off if _____

Things that get me really angry are _____

These are my good and bad habits _____

_____

I wish that I could change the way I _____

The things that I would like to change in other people are _____

_____

The proudest moment of my life _____

I will some day _____

The TV show I enjoy watching _____

The best movie that I have ever seen _____

_____

This is how I feel about school _____

_____

_____

About Me!

I sometimes wish _____

_____

I often learn best if _____

_____

It is difficult for me to learn when _____

_____

My role model is _____

If I had three wishes, they would be _____

_____

_____

My accomplishments are _____

I enjoy _____

_____

I am happy when _____

The most important person in my life is _____

I get frustrated when _____

_____

My biggest goal is to _____

The nicest thing I ever did _____

_____

My favorite subjects are _____

The subjects I don't enjoy are _____

When I look at myself in the mirror what I see is _____

_____

_____

There is something else I could tell you about me _____

_____

_____

_____

STUDENT TIMETABLE

NAME ....

HOMEROOM ....

Period	Day 1	Day 2	Day 3	Day 4	Day 5	Day 6

Certificate of Achievement

This certifies that

has successfully

_____

_____

_____

Signature _____ Date _____

THANK YOU!

TO: _____

FOR: _____

_____

_____

TEACHER: _____

DATE: _____

THANK YOU!

TO: _____

FOR: _____

_____

_____

TEACHER: _____

DATE: _____

THANK YOU!

TO: _____

FOR: _____

_____

_____

TEACHER: _____

DATE: _____

Name ....

1. ....   3. ....

2. ....   4. ....

Color or mark a square each time the above goals have been reached.   Reward

TODAY'S GOALS

*My **goals** for today are:*

1. _____

2. _____

3. _____

*To **make my goals** I will need to do the following:* _____

_____

_____

_____

*I **have** made my goals!* ☐

*My **new goals** for tomorrow will be:*

1. _____

2. _____

3. _____

*I **have not** made my goals.* ☐

*The **new strategy** that I will try next time will be:*

_____

_____

_____

Signature: _____

Date: _____

Witness: _____

THIS WEEK'S GOALS

*My **goals** for this week are:*

1. _____
2. _____
3. _____

*Some **possible obstacles** to making my goals are* _____

_____

_____

*To **make my goals** I need to do the following:* _____

_____

_____

_____

*I **have** made my goals!* ☐

*My **new goals** for next week are:*

1. _____
2. _____
3. _____

*I **have not** made my goals.* ☐

*The **new strategy** that I will try next week will be* _____

_____

_____

_____

Signature: _____

Date: _____

Witness: _____

STUDENT CONTRACT

I, _____ , **agree to** undertake the following

responsibilities to the best of my ability: _____

_____

_____

_____

_____

_____

In return for a successful completion of the above stated responsibilities I will receive

the following **privileges:**

1._____

_____

2. _____

_____

3. _____

_____

The contract will be binding to both parties from _____ to_____

CONTRACT **REVIEW** DATE: _____

Date signed: _____

Student Signature: _____

Teacher Signature: _____

© 1996 Good Apple

GOAL ACHIEVED!

Hooray, I achieved my goal! The goal was _____

_____

I did it by doing the following: _____

_____

The most difficult part was _____

_____

These are some of the things that I have learned
about myself as I tried to achieve my goal: _____

_____

_____

_____

Making my goal was important because: _____

_____

_____

Signed: _____

Dated: _____

✂ -

GOAL ACHIEVED!

Hooray, I achieved my goal! The goal was _____

_____

I did it by doing the following: _____

_____

The most difficult part was _____

_____

These are some of the things that I have learned
about myself as I tried to achieve my goal: _____

_____

_____

_____

Making my goal was important because: _____

_____

_____

Signed: _____

Dated: _____

WEEKLY BEHAVIOR

STUDENT'S NAME: _____

TEACHER: _____   CLASS: _____

WEEK OF _____ TO _____

BEHAVIORAL GOALS

1. _____
2. _____
3. _____
4. _____

PLACE A ✓ IN EACH SQUARE WHERE ONE OF THE ABOVE GOALS HAS BEEN ACHIEVED.

STUDENT'S COMMENTS

_____
_____
_____
_____
_____
_____
_____
_____

PERIOD	1	2	3	4	5	6	7	8
MONDAY								
TUESDAY								
WEDNESDAY								
THURSDAY								
FRIDAY								

DAILY PROGRESS REPORT

Student's Name: _____ Class: _____

Teacher: _____ Date: _____

PERIOD/SUBJECT	TEACHER'S COMMENTS	HOMEWORK ASSIGNED	STUDENT'S COMMENTS

Parent's Comments

Signature: _____

WEEKLY PROGRESS REPORT

Student's Name: _____ Class: _____

Teacher: _____ Week of: _____ to _____

MONDAY	TUESDAY	WEDNESDAY	THURSDAY	FRIDAY

SUMMARY:

PARENT'S COMMENTS:

SIGNATURE: _____

ASSIGNMENT NOT DONE!

Please be informed that _____ has **not** completed the following assignment:

Subject:	
Assignment Date:	
Due Date:	

Assignment: _____

_____

Teacher: _____

Parent Signature: _____ Date: _____

✂ --

ASSIGNMENT NOT DONE!

Please be informed that _____ has **not** completed the following assignment:

Subject:	
Assignment Date:	
Due Date:	

Assignment: _____

_____

Teacher: _____

Parent Signature: _____ Date: _____

PROBLEM REPORT

Date: _____

Student Name: _____

Time of Incident: _____

Describe what happened in detail. **What** did you do and **why** did you do it?

_____

_____

_____

_____

_____

_____

Who else **witnessed** the incident? _____

Who was **hurt** by what you did? _____

_____

What **strategies** could you have used to avoid the situation?

_____

_____

_____

_____

_____

Teacher's Comments: _____

_____

_____

_____

Parent's Comments: _____

_____

_____

_____

Parent's Signature: _____   Teacher's Signature: _____

PLACE VALUE CHART

NAME: _____

CLASS: _____

Billions			Millions			Thousands			Ones			Less Than One		
H	T	O	H	T	O	H	T	O	H	T	O	T	H	TH

MULTIPLICATION TABLES
TO 12

	1	2	3	4	5	6	7	8	9	10	11	12
1	1	2	3	4	5	6	7	8	9	10	11	12
2	2	4	6	8	10	12	14	16	18	20	22	24
3	3	6	9	12	15	18	21	24	27	30	33	36
4	4	8	12	16	20	24	28	32	36	40	44	48
5	5	10	15	20	25	30	35	40	45	50	55	60
6	6	12	18	24	30	36	42	48	54	60	66	72
7	7	14	21	28	35	42	49	56	63	70	77	84
8	8	16	24	32	40	48	56	64	72	80	88	96
9	9	18	27	36	45	54	63	72	81	90	99	108
10	10	20	30	40	50	60	70	80	90	100	110	120
11	11	22	33	44	55	66	77	88	99	110	121	132
12	12	24	36	48	60	72	84	96	108	120	132	144

MULTIPLICATION TABLES

	1	2	3	4	5	6	7	8	9	10	11	12
1												
2												
3												
4												
5												
6												
7												
8												
9												
10												
11												
12												

MULTIPLICATION FACTS RECORD

Student's Name	2x	3x	4x	5x	6x	7x	8x	9x	10x	11x	12x

TEMPERATURE CONVERSION

$$T°F = (1.8T + 32)°C \qquad T°C = \left(\frac{T-32}{1.8}\right)°F$$

C°	F°	C°	F°
-40	-40	120	248
-30	-22	130	266
-20	-4	140	284
-15	5	150	302
-10	14	160	320
-5	23	170	338
0	32	180	356
5	41	190	374
10	50	200	392
15	59	210	410
20	68	220	428
30	86	230	446
40	104	240	464
50	122	250	482
60	140	260	500
70	158	270	518
80	176	280	536
90	194	290	554
100	212	300	572
110	230	500	932

THE METRIC SYSTEM

LENGTH

Kilometer	Hectometer	Decameter	Meter	Decimeter	Centimeter	Millimeter
km	hm	dam	m	dm	cm	mm
1000m	100m	10m	1m	0.1m	0.01m	0.001m

MASS

Kilogram	Hectogram	Decagram	Gram	Decigram	Centigram	Milligram
kg	hg	dag	g	dg	cg	mg
1000g	100g	10g	1g	0.1g	0.01g	0.001g

CAPACITY

Kiloliter	Hectoliter	Decaliter	Liter	Deciliter	Centiliter	Milliliter
kL	hL	daL	L	dL	cL	mL
1000L	100L	10L	1L	0.1L	0.01L	0.001L

ROMAN NUMERALS

1	**I**	one	24	**XXIV**	twenty-four
2	**II**	two	25	**XXV**	twenty-five
3	**III**	three	26	**XXVI**	twenty-six
4	**IV**	four	27	**XXVII**	twenty-seven
5	**V**	five	28	**XXVIII**	twenty-eight
6	**VI**	six	29	**XXIX**	twenty-nine
7	**VII**	seven	30	**XXX**	thirty
8	**VIII**	eight	40	**XL**	forty
9	**IX**	nine	50	**L**	fifty
10	**X**	ten	60	**LX**	sixty
11	**XI**	eleven	70	**LXX**	seventy
12	**XII**	twelve	80	**LXXX**	eighty
13	**XIII**	thirteen	90	**XC**	ninety
14	**XIV**	fourteen	100	**C**	one hundred
15	**XV**	fifteen	200	**CC**	two hundred
16	**XVI**	sixteen	300	**CCC**	three hundred
17	**XVII**	seventeen	400	**CD**	four hundred
18	**XVIII**	eighteen	500	**D**	five hundred
19	**XIX**	nineteen	600	**DC**	six hundred
20	**XX**	twenty	700	**DCC**	seven hundred
21	**XXI**	twenty-one	800	**DCCC**	eight hundred
22	**XXII**	twenty-two	900	**CM**	nine hundred
23	**XXIII**	twenty-three	1000	**M**	one thousand

INCH GRID

NAME: _____

NAME: _____

NAME: _____

MAKE YOUR OWN GRAPHS

NAME: _____

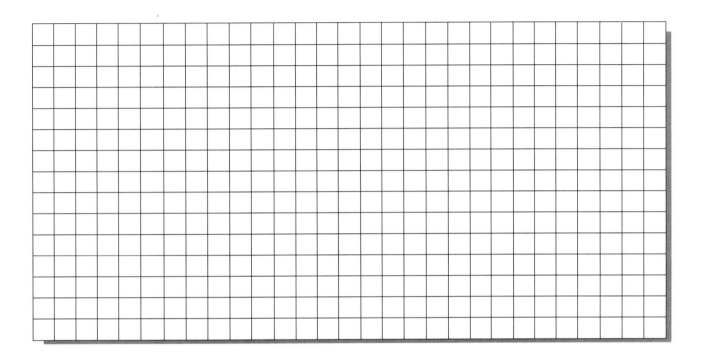

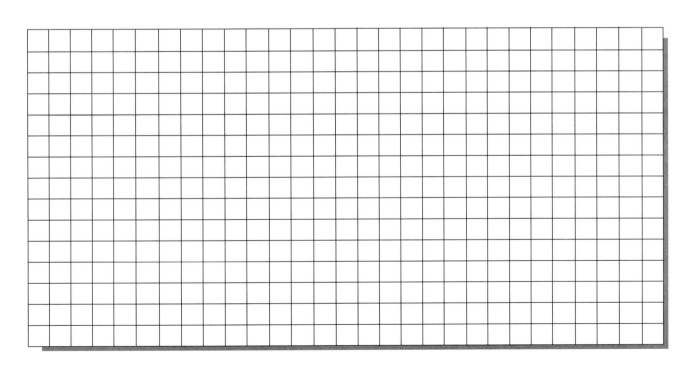

MAKE YOUR OWN
GRAPH

NAME: _____

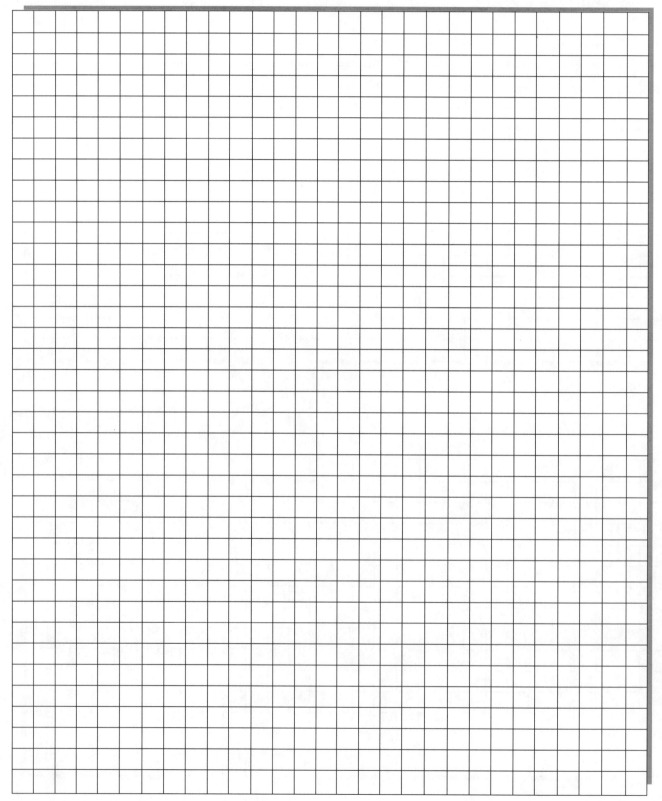

Subtopic

Subtopic

Subtopic

Subtopic

Main Topic

Subtopic

Subtopic

Subtopic

Subtopic

NEWSPAPER ACTIVITY

NAME: _____

Read the selected newspaper article or story twice. In the space below, describe the basic facts. Be prepared to share your work with the class.

WHO? (Who is the story about? List names, titles, and ages of individuals.)

_____
_____
_____

WHAT? (Describe exactly what happened. What is the story mainly about?)

_____
_____
_____
_____
_____
_____
_____
_____
_____

WHERE? (Where did the story take place? Clearly state the location.)

_____
_____

WHEN? (When did it happen? Be specific. Include day, date, and time.)

_____

WHY or HOW? (Why and how did it happen? Use back if necessary.)

_____
_____
_____
_____
_____

PROOFREADING CHECKLIST

Use this checklist to help you proofread your rough draft. This process will ensure that your published work is free of simple errors. When done, ask one other person to proofread your work as well.

Work Title: _____

Proofreader (Use ✓ or ?)	#1	#2
1. My work has a correctly spelled title.		
2. My writing is well spaced and legible.		
3. I have underlined (circled) and then corrected all my spelling errors.		
4. Each of my sentences is a complete thought.		
5. I have checked for the correct use of the following: ▲ Periods		
▲ Commas		
▲ Apostrophes		
▲ Quotation marks		
6. I have capitalized the following: ▲ Names of people and places		
▲ Beginning of each sentence		
▲ Names of days, months, and holidays		
▲ Important title words		
7. I have remembered to write using paragraph style.		
8. My ideas are easy to understand.		

Name _____   Proofreader _____

Use the blank pages of this sheet to help you *plan* your illustrated story. Create simple. *rough* drawings.

FRONT COVER   **ABOUT THE AUTHOR**   **TITLE PAGE**

MY
STORYBOARD

Illustration

BACK COVER

COMMON SPELLING RULES

DOUBLE THE FINAL CONSONANT

▲ Double the final consonant in a word that ends in a single consonant preceded by a vowel when adding a suffix beginning with a vowel.

Examples: beg**in** + ing = begi**nn**ing,   jo**g** + ed = jo**gg**ed

DROP THE SILENT E

▲ Drop the **silent e** when adding a suffix beginning with a vowel to a word ending in a silent e.

Examples: Writ**e** + ing = writing,   fam**e** + ous = famous

KEEP THE SILENT E

▲ Keep the **silent e** when adding the suffix **able, ance,** or **ous** to a word ending in soft **ce** or **ge.**

Examples: notic**e** + **able** = noticeable,   courag**e** + **ous** = courageous

▲ Keep the **silent e,** as well, when adding a suffix beginning with a consonant to a word ending in **silent e.**

Examples: complet**e** + ly = complet**e**ly,   saf**e** + ty = saf**e**ty

CHANGE THE Y TO I

▲ Change the **y** to **i** when adding a suffix to a word ending in a **y** preceded by a consonant.

Examples: lonel**y** + **ness** = lonel**i**ness,   eas**y** + ly = eas**i**ly

I BEFORE E EXCEPT AFTER C

▲ Place **i** before **e** except after **c.** In other words, place **e** before **i** after **c.**
This rule works in words in which **i** and **e** are pronounced as **ee.**

Examples: bel**ie**ve, ach**ie**ve, rece**i**ve, rece**i**pt, y**ie**ld, th**ie**f, n**ie**ce

E BEFORE I

▲ If the pronunciation of **ei** is a long **a,** place **e** before **i.**

Examples: sl**ei**gh, w**ei**ght, r**ei**gn, n**ei**ghbor, fr**ei**ght

NEW WORDS

Improve your vocabulary by finding the meanings of
new words. In the space provided, record each unfamiliar
word and its common meaning and sentence use.

NAME: _____

WORD	MEANING	SENTENCE USE
1.		
2.		
3.		
4.		
5.		
6.		
7.		
8.		
9.		
10.		

FREQUENTLY MISSPELLED WORDS

a lot
ache
again
almost
always
answer
appear
because
been
before
beginning
believe
below
blue
break
build
business
busy
buy
cannot
can't
caught
chief
choose
clothes
coming
cough
could
couldn't
decide

desert
develop
didn't
die
early
easy
eight
enough
every
February
flew
flight
fly
forty
four
fourth
friend
fruit
government
guess
guest
half
hear
heard
here
hole
hour
I'd
I'll
I'm

instead
isn't
it's
I've
knew
know
knowledge
laid
language
length
lie
loose
lose
lying
meant
measure
minute
misspell
necessary
none
o'clock
once
peace
piece
raise
receive
right
route
said
says

science
seems
separate
shoes
sight
since
some
somewhere
straight
suite
sure
sweat
sweet
tear
their
there
therefore
they
they're
they've
though
thought
threw
through
throw
tired
tonight
too
trouble
truly

Tuesday
twelve
two
used
very
wasn't
wear
weather
week
weight
were
we're
where
whether
which
who
who's
whole
whose
women
won't
would
wouldn't
write
writing
wrote
you'll
you're
you've
your

MY MISSPELLED WORDS

NAME: _____   DATE: _____

1. _____	16. _____	31. _____	46. _____
2. _____	17. _____	32. _____	47. _____
3. _____	18. _____	33. _____	48. _____
4. _____	19. _____	34. _____	49. _____
5. _____	20. _____	35. _____	50. _____
6. _____	21. _____	36. _____	51. _____
7. _____	22. _____	37. _____	52. _____
8. _____	23. _____	38. _____	53. _____
9. _____	24. _____	39. _____	54. _____
10. _____	25. _____	40. _____	55. _____
11. _____	26. _____	41. _____	56. _____
12. _____	27. _____	42. _____	57. _____
13. _____	28. _____	43. _____	58. _____
14. _____	29. _____	44. _____	59. _____
15. _____	30. _____	45. _____	60. _____

WORD SEARCH

TOPIC: _____

NAME: _____

1. _____   13. _____

2. _____   14. _____

3. _____   15. _____

4. _____   16. _____

5. _____   17. _____

6. _____   18. _____

7. _____   19. _____

8. _____   20. _____

9. _____   21. _____

10. _____   22. _____

11. _____   23. _____

12. _____   24. _____

COMMON WORD ENDINGS

-ANT
abundant
distant
instant

-ANCE
abundance
distance
instance

-ENT
confident
dependent
silent

-ENCE
confidence
dependence
silence

-ABLE
available
believable
changeable

-IBLE
digestible
flexible
sensible

-ARY
dictionary
honorary
imaginary

-ERY
archery
bravery
lottery

-ORY
circulatory
laboratory
• sensory

-DOM
freedom
kingdom
wisdom

-ER
laborer
manager
teacher

-IAN
comedian
electrician
politician

-MENT
accomplishment
disappointment
equipment

-NESS
friendliness
happiness
loneliness

-OR
creator
mediator
spectator

-TURE
fixture
mixture
signature

-URE
adventure
creature
moisture

-ATION
aviation
information
reservation

-ION
communion
complexion
opinion

-ITION
addition
competition
repetition

-SION
collision
confession
television

-TION
action
attraction
education

-IOUS
furious
mysterious
rebellious

-OUS
disastrous
joyous
nervous

-ISE
advertise
exercise

-IZE
apologize
memorize

-LESS
pointless
careless

COMMON PREFIXES

MEANING: NOT

a-	dis-
aseptic	disappear
asymmetrical	discourage
atypical	dislike

il-	im-
illegal	immoral
illegible	impossible
illogical	impure

in-	ir-
inaccurate	irrational
inexperienced	irrefutable
incoherent	irregular

non-	un-
nonaligned	uncomfortable
nonconformist	unconditional
nonprofit	unconscious
nonsense	undecided

NUMBERS

uni- (one, single)	bi- (two, double)
unicorn	bicentennial
unicycle	bicycle
unison	bifocal

tri- (three)	semi- (half, partly)
triangle	semiannual
triceps	semicircle
tricycle	semiconscious

DIRECTION

inter- (between, among)	
intercept	international
interfere	interplanetary

sub- (under)	
submarine	subtitle
submerge	subtract

trans- (across, over, beyond)	
transform	transplant
transfusion	transport

OPPOSITE PREFIXES

pro- & anti-

pro- (forward in space and time, in support of)	
procedure	progress
produce	project

anti- (against, opposite, or opposed)	
antibiotic	antifreeze
antidote	antisocial

pre- & post-

pre- (before)	
preamble	precede
prearrange	predecessor
precaution	predict

post- (after)	
postdate	postnatal
postgraduate	postpone
posthumous	postscript

ADJECTIVE

Any word that modifies, describes, or adds to the meaning of a noun.
Examples: The <u>old</u> man wore a <u>blue</u> hat.

ADVERB

Any word that describes or adds to the meaning of a verb, adjective, or other adverb.
An adverb tells how, why, when, where, and in what manner an action takes place.
Examples: The baby cried <u>impatiently</u> as his mother <u>hurriedly</u> went to get his milk bottle.
The students ran <u>quickly</u> to their classrooms.

CONJUNCTION

Conjunctions are joining or linking words. There are two types of conjunctions.
Coordinating conjunctions: These connect sentence parts equal in rank, single words, phrases, or clauses. They are the following: **and, but, yet, or, nor, for, so, both, not only, either,** and **neither.**
Example: Study tonight<u>, and</u> tomorrow you will feel ready for the math test.
Subordinating conjunctions: These join two clauses, the main and the subordinate (dependent) clause. It is a joining word that expresses a relationship between two ideas that are not equal in rank. One idea can stand as a sentence, whereas the one introduced by the subordinating conjunction cannot stand as a sentence by itself. Some examples are **after, though, as long as, as soon as, because, before, even though, once, since, until,** and so forth.
Example: <u>Although</u> you don't deserve it, I will continue to help you with your homework.

NOUN

Words that name people, places, and things.
Proper nouns: name specific people, places, and things. These words should be capitalized.
Examples: **Laura, Mississippi, Thursday, Easter**
Common nouns: refer to general names for a number of things, such as **father, house, boy.**

PRONOUN

Words that may be used in place of nouns. **I, you, he, she, it, we,** and **they,** are some examples.
Examples: <u>They</u> went to fix <u>it</u> as soon as <u>he</u> gave them the permission.

VERB

Words that show action or a state of being. (The man <u>nodded</u> his head because he was content.)

PREPOSITION

Words that show how a noun or pronoun relates to another word. They often indicate position.
Example: He placed his sword <u>on</u> the ground.
Into, at, behind, above, before, near, toward, under, and **beside** are other examples of prepositions.

APOSTROPHE '

Use an apostrophe to show possession with a proper noun, common noun, indefinite pronoun, period of time, and sum of money. An apostrophe is also used to act as a placeholder for a missing letter and when constructing contractions.

Examples: (a) Laura's science notebook (b) Anyone's guess (c) Today's proverb (d) Seven dollar's worth (e) Fun 'n' games (f) He isn't here.

COLON :

Use a colon to introduce a list, to introduce an end portion of a sentence that is an explanation, after an introductory classification, and after the salutation in a business letter.

Examples: (a) Supplies: (list follows) (b) I learned the following: My skills were rusty and I was out of shape. (c) The Sahara made me think of one thing: water! (d) Dear Mr. Dobs:

SEMICOLON ;

Use a semicolon to lengthen or expand an original thought, to group items in series that contain commas, and in compound sentences preceding the adverbs *then, however, thus, hence, indeed, accordingly, besides,* and *therefore.*

Examples: (a) My new strategy did not work; the attempt to win by irritating my opponent had failed entirely. (b) His family has homes in Bar Harbor, Maine; Paris, France; and Detroit, Michigan. (c) She wants to major in French; however, she can't meet the requirements.

PERIOD, EXCLAMATION MARK, QUESTION MARK . ! ?

Every written sentence must end with a period, exclamation mark, or question mark. A period marks the end of a normal sentence that is not a question and is not emphatic. It is also placed at the end of an abbreviation. An exclamation mark is used at the end of sentences in which the writer means to show strong emphasis or emotion. A question mark is used to close a question.

COMMA ,

Use a comma to separate all items in a series; between two independent clauses joined by *and, but, or, nor, for, yet,* or *so*; with appositives (nouns that repeat, explain, or stand in for other nouns); and after introductory adverbial phrases.

Examples: (a) The flag is green, brown, and white. (b) I'd love to go with you, but I have to clean up my room. (c) Chloe, my dog, is black and white. (d) After the appetizer and soup, we were too full for the main course!

QUOTATION MARKS " "

Use quotation marks to enclose a direct quotation. Commas and periods go *inside* closing quotation marks. Exclamation marks and question marks go inside closing quotation marks if they are part of the original quotation; otherwise, they go outside.

Example: (a) "Please feed the dog," said mother. (b) "Clean your room!" ordered his father. (c) Did you really say, "Absolutely not"?

CONTRACTIONS

A contraction is a shortened form of two words. It is created when one or more letters are removed and replaced by an apostrophe. Contractions are most often used in informal or semiformal writing.

CONTRACTION	Comes from
doesn't	does not
don't	do not
hadn't	had not
hasn't	has not
haven't	have not
he'd	he would, he had
he's	he is, he has
here's	here is
I'll	I will
I'm	I am
I've	I have
isn't	is not
it'll	it will
it's	it is, it has
let's	let us
mustn't	must not
she'd	she would, she had

CONTRACTION	Comes from
she's	she is, she has
shouldn't	should not
that's	that is
they'd	they would, they had
they'll	they will
they're	they are
they've	they have
you'd	you would, you had
you'll	you will
you're	you are
you've	you have
we'd	we would, we had
we've	we have
where's	where is, where has
who's	who is, who has
wouldn't	would not
won't	will not

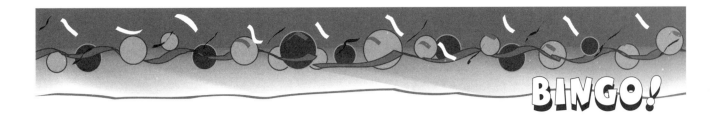

BINGO!

NAME: _____

		FREE		

SUBSTITUTE SURVIVAL KIT

Welcome to our class! I hope that your visit will be a rewarding and meaningful experience both to the students and you. Here is some information you may find helpful.

Teacher:_____ Class: _____ Room # _____

Principal: _____ School:_____

Secretary: _____

▲ My lesson plans are located _____

▲ You may contact the office by _____

▲ School schedule:

a.m.			p.m.		
Arrival Time:			Arrival Time:	
Announcements:			Period 5:	
Period 1:			Period 6:	
Period 2:			Period 7:	
Period 3:			Period 8:	
Period 4:			Dismissal:	
Lunch:			Other Activities:	

▲ My seating plan is located_____

▲ Class attendance lists can be found _____

▲ Attendance procedures: _____

_____

▲ Our attendance monitor is _____

▲ Yard, hall, and other duties: _____

_____

_____

▲ The following students can be approached for further assistance:

_____

▲ If you need additional help, please contact _____in room _____

CLASSROOM PROCEDURES

Class Entry: _____
_____
_____
_____

Monitors: _____

Daily Routines: _____
_____
_____
_____
_____
_____
_____

Materials: _____
_____

Our Rules & Consequences: _____
_____
_____
_____
_____
_____

Lunch: _____
_____

Dismissal: _____
_____
_____

Other: _____
_____
_____

SEATING PLAN

SPECIAL NEEDS LIST

The following list will inform you about some of my students' special needs. Please consider each carefully when deciding on the way you will implement the given daily lesson plans.

STUDENT NAME   **SPECIAL NEEDS**

TODAY'S LESSON PLAN

DAY .... **DATE** ....

PERIOD .... **CLASS** .... **ROOM**	**SUPPLIES NEEDED**

ASSIGNED HOMEWORK :

PHOTOCOPY:

PERIOD .... **CLASS** .... **ROOM**	**SUPPLIES NEEDED**

ASSIGNED HOMEWORK :

PHOTOCOPY:

SUPERVISION DUTIES:

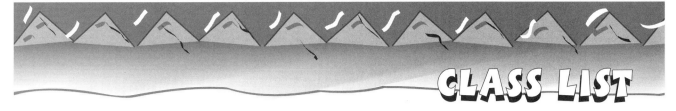

CLASS LIST

TEACHER ....**CLASS** ....**ROOM** ....

Name	Phone No.	Date of Birth	Age	Locker Number/Combination

END-OF-DAY
SUMMARY

Thank you for teaching and caring for my class in my absence. Please take a moment to write a note summarizing your experience. List any behaviors (positive and negative) that you may have encountered. Once again, thank you for your help and support.

Teacher: _____

_____

_____

_____

_____

_____

_____

_____

_____

_____

_____

_____

_____

_____

_____

_____

_____

_____

_____

_____

_____

_____

_____

Substitute Teacher's Name: _____ Date: _____

LIBRARY PASS

Class: _____
Students: _____
_____
_____

Assignment: *Personal Use* ☐ *Book Selection* ☐ ✓
Research Topic: _____
Additional Instructions: _____
_____

Time Sent: _____ Return Time: _____
Teacher: _____

LIBRARY PASS

Class: _____
Students: _____
_____
_____

Assignment: *Personal Use* ☐ *Book Selection* ☐ ✓
Research Topic: _____
Additional Instructions: _____
_____

Time Sent: _____ Return Time: _____
Teacher: _____

LIBRARY PASS

Class: _____
Students: _____
_____
_____

Assignment: *Personal Use* ☐ *Book Selection* ☐ ✓
Research Topic: _____
Additional Instructions: _____
_____

Time Sent: _____ Return Time: _____
Teacher: _____

LIBRARY PASS

Class: _____
Students: _____
_____
_____

Assignment: *Personal Use* ☐ *Book Selection* ☐ ✓
Research Topic: _____
Additional Instructions: _____
_____

Time Sent: _____ Return Time: _____
Teacher: _____

LIBRARY PASS

Class: _____
Students: _____
_____
_____

Assignment: *Personal Use* ☐ *Book Selection* ☐ ✓
Research Topic: _____
Additional Instructions: _____
_____

Time Sent: _____ Return Time: _____
Teacher: _____

LIBRARY PASS

Class: _____
Students: _____
_____
_____

Assignment: *Personal Use* ☐ *Book Selection* ☐ ✓
Research Topic: _____
Additional Instructions: _____
_____

Time Sent: _____ Return Time: _____
Teacher: _____

HALL PASS

HALL PASS

NAME: _____ DATE: _____

CLASS: _____ ROOM: _____

REASON: _____

TIME SENT: _____

TIME RETURNED: _____

SIGNATURE: _____

HALL PASS

NAME: _____ DATE: _____

CLASS: _____ ROOM: _____

REASON: _____

TIME SENT: _____

TIME RETURNED: _____

SIGNATURE: _____

HALL PASS

NAME: _____ DATE: _____

CLASS: _____ ROOM: _____

REASON: _____

TIME SENT: _____

TIME RETURNED: _____

SIGNATURE: _____

HALL PASS

NAME: _____ DATE: _____

CLASS: _____ ROOM: _____

REASON: _____

TIME SENT: _____

TIME RETURNED: _____

SIGNATURE: _____

HALL PASS

NAME: _____ DATE: _____

CLASS: _____ ROOM: _____

REASON: _____

TIME SENT: _____

TIME RETURNED: _____

SIGNATURE: _____

HALL PASS

NAME: _____ DATE: _____

CLASS: _____ ROOM: _____

REASON: _____

TIME SENT: _____

TIME RETURNED: _____

SIGNATURE: _____

HALL PASS

NAME: _____ DATE: _____

CLASS: _____ ROOM: _____

REASON: _____

TIME SENT: _____

TIME RETURNED: _____

SIGNATURE: _____

HALL PASS

NAME: _____ DATE: _____

CLASS: _____ ROOM: _____

REASON: _____

TIME SENT: _____

TIME RETURNED: _____

SIGNATURE: _____

AUDIOVISUAL BOOKING

Date: _____

period	1	2	3	4	5	6	7
VCR #1							
Name							
Room #							
VCR #2							
Name							
Room #							
VCR #3							
Name							
Room #							
camcorder							
Name							
Room #							
film projector							
Name							
Room #							
Name							
Room #							

TITLE: _____ **TEACHER:** _____

STUDENT NAME					

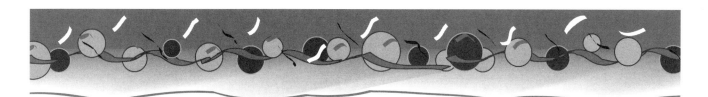

TOPIC: _____   **NAME:** _____

_____

_____

_____

_____

_____

_____

_____

_____

_____

_____

_____

_____

_____

_____

_____

_____

_____

_____

_____

_____

_____

_____

_____

_____

_____

_____

_____

_____

_____

_____

_____

STAFF PAPER

Name: _____

Class: _____ Teacher: _____